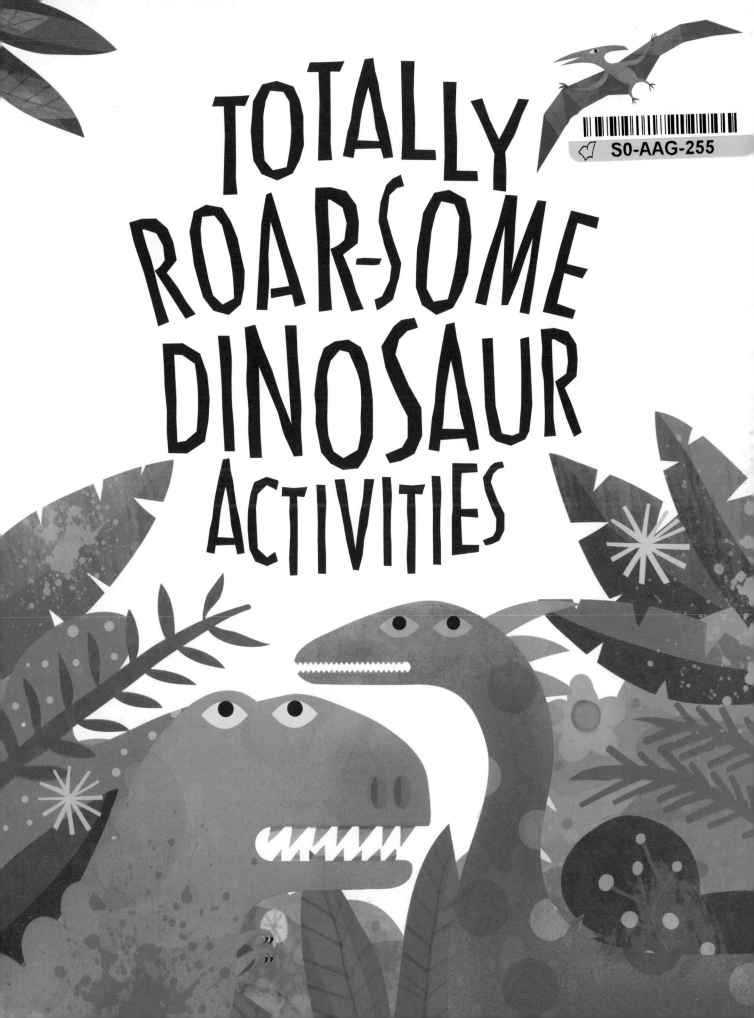

TOTALLY ROAR-SOME DINOSAUR ACTIVITIES

This edition published by Parragon Books Ltd in 2017
and distributed by

Parragon Inc.
440 Park Avenue South, 13th Floor
New York, NY 10016
www.parragon.com

Written by Mandy Archer
Illustrated by Gareth Lucas
Designed by Kate Wakeham and 38a The Shop

ISBN 978-1-4748-1464-5

Printed in China

TOTALLY ROAR-SOME DINOSAUR ACTIVITIES

PaRragon

Bath · New York · Cologne · Melbourne · Delhi
Hong Kong · Shenzhen · Singapore

Who's hatching?

Uh-oh ...
Here comes mama dinosaur!

Yikes!

We need spots, scales, spikes, and stripes.

Can you fill the gaps in this picture?
Find the right puzzle pieces, then copy them into the frame.

Peeping dino,
keep your cool.
What is lurking
in the pool?

This Stegosaurus looks seriously silly!
Add a row of dino plates along his back.

Buzz, buzz, buzz ... gulp!

Who will be eaten?

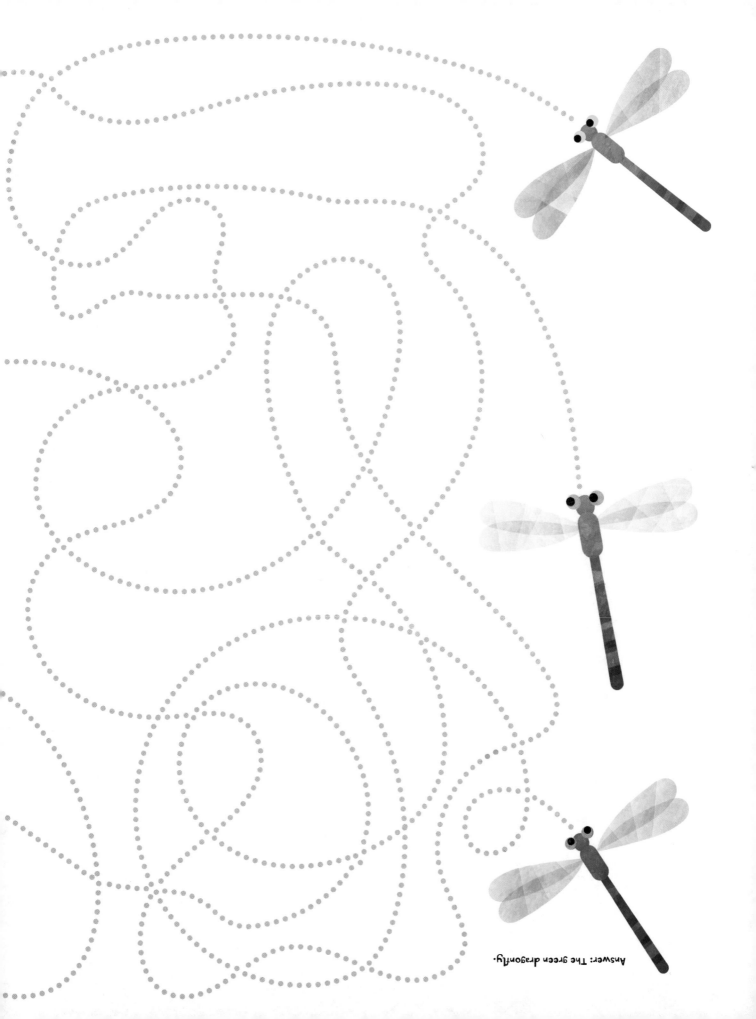

Answer: The green dragonfly.

What's up? Fill the sky with soaring Pterosaurs.

Now make these volcanoes **bubble** and **blow.**

This ocean swirls with fearsome fish...

...and slippery squid!

Use the number key to color in these underwater friends.

1 2 3 4 5 6

Turn this tiny twosome into a huge, happy herd.

Use your pen to unleash a snapping, snarling pack of dinos!

Spinosaurus is searching for her identical twin.

Use greens and blues to bring her spiny sister to life.

Gaze at the rows of scaly toes . . .
doodle the dinosaurs that they belong to!

An enormous dinosaur
lurks in this cave! Use your artist's
imagination to bring him into the light.

RO ar!

Who, or what, is making that noise?

Color the scales of this
SCARY T. rex!

Color in the shadows to complete this dinosaur pattern.

START

Baby Triceratops needs to find his way to the watering hole!

Whose hole is this?

Can you find . . .

something prickly . . .

. . . and something smooth?

Put crocs
on the
rocks!

How many frogs can you find?

Answer: 6 frogs.

Use your sketching skills to put the dinosaurs back in the picture!

Add ...

4 x

3 x

2 x

1 x

What a lot of dino babies!

Make every tiny Triceratops look different from its brothers and sisters.

Mama dinosaur's babies look just like her!
Sketch seven teeny T. rexes
snapping their tiny teeth.

Draw some eye-popping dinosaur tails.

Will they be spiky, silly, or slithery?

What is lurking in the water? Join the dots,
then color in the creatures of the deep.

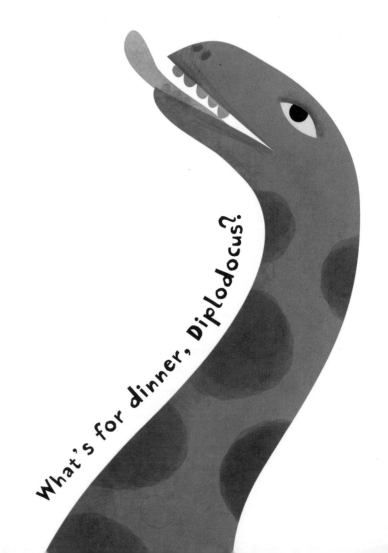

What's for dinner, Diplodocus?

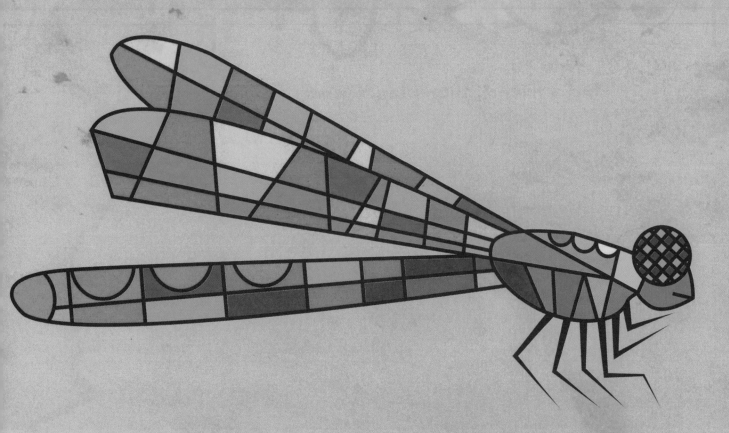

Match the dragonfly's rainbow colors.

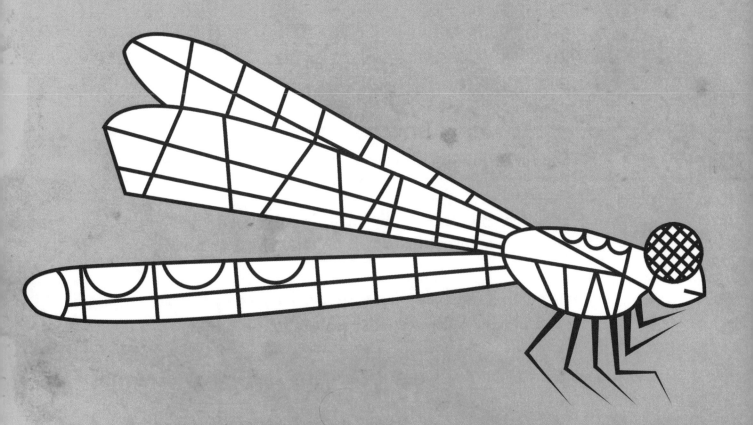

Find a friend, then play a game of swamp squares!

HOW TO PLAY
Take turns joining up two dots on the game board.

Every time you draw a line that completes a square,
write your initial inside, then take another turn.

Keep going until all of the squares are completed.
The player with the most points is the winner.

Empty square = 1 POINT   = 2 POINTS   = 5 POINTS

Peep into the cave, then draw the eyes ...
if you dare!

Camouflage these little dinosaurs in the jungle!

What's in T. rex's
mouth?

Doodle dinosaurs
meeting at the
water's edge!

Which two green dinos are exactly the same?

Tickly tentacles! Draw more ammonites swimming in their shells.

Thud!

Thud!

Thud!

Thud!

Who are these tiny, timid dinosaurs running away from?

Who's chasing who?
Add some more
dizzy dinosaurs!

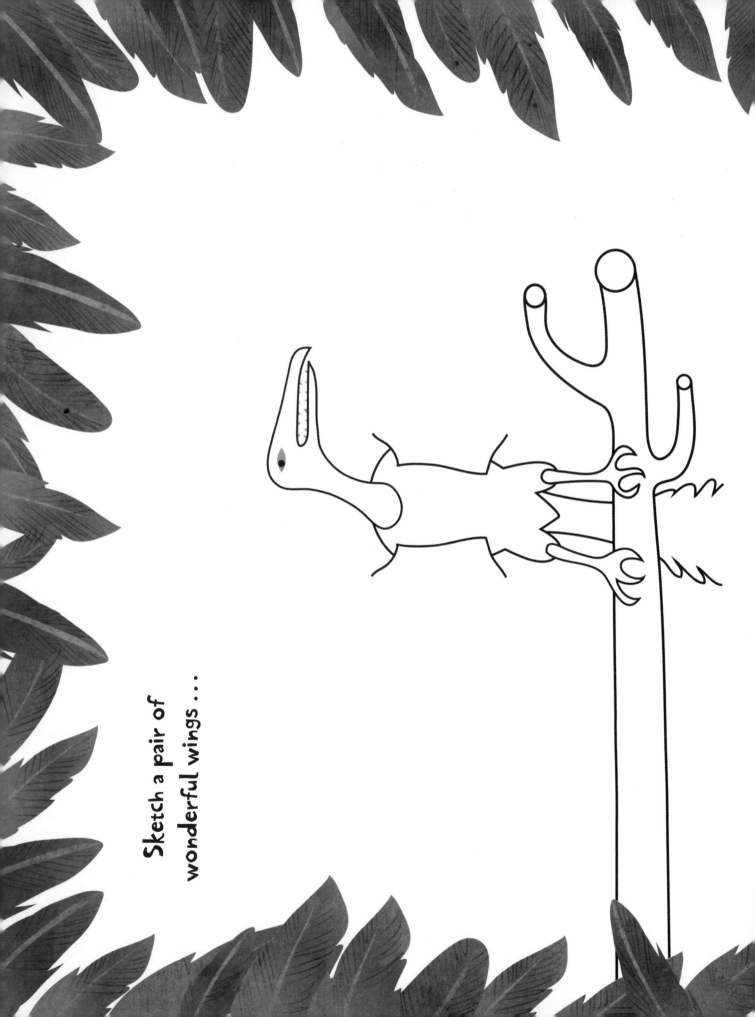

Sketch a pair of wonderful wings . . .

... then add a stunning
plume of tail feathers!

Six sneaky dinosaurs are hiding in the forest. Find the first one, then draw five more.

Never wake a sleeping dinosaur!

Fill his head with dinosaur dreams instead.

Triceratops rock!

Find and circle five differences between these two pictures.

wHiiiiiirrrr! The air is alive with dragonflies!

How many have . . .

YELLOW EYES   STRIPY BODIES   BLUE WINGS

Add fearsome faces, flashing eyes, and terrible teeth.

Fill the frames with your best dinosaur doodles!

A creature from the deep

A tough Triceratops

A cracking dinosaur egg

Have your pencils ready!

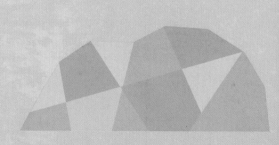

A swooping Pterosaur

A dramatic dragonfly

a massive
Giganotosaurus!

Dotty shapes, lurking lumps,
Draw the dino's humps and bumps!.

Fill the sky with
flying friends.

Give this dinosaur a frill to be proud of.

Now you've met the dinosaur babies . . . draw Mom and Dad!

Phew! It gets hot in the desert.

Draw the details to finish these twins.

Now sketch
some more
fierce friends,
scuttling around
the page.

Who has
left these
messy trails?

How many dinosaurs
are in the herd?

Turn over for
the answer!

When you've finished with the other side of this page, make a Triceratops mask!
(There were 31 dinosaurs in the herd!)

Color in the face, then ask a grown-up to help you cut it out and stick it onto some white cardboard, and to cut along all the dotted lines.

Press a pen through the black dots on each side of the mask, to make a hole each side. Tie a piece of elastic through each hole. Use this to attach the mask to your head.

Ready? It's time to dinosaur ROAR!

What a lot of dotty dinosaurs! Trace the dots, add patterns and color.

START

It's easy to get lost in the swamp.
Help the dinosaur find his friend.

FINISH

Who is chasing the little
yellow dinosaur?

Find all of the little pictures in the big picture.

Yum! What have you eaten?

This dinosaur likes munching leaves. Color these trees.

Who is tall enough
to nibble the top
of this tree?

Use your coloring skills to make the dinosaurs match.

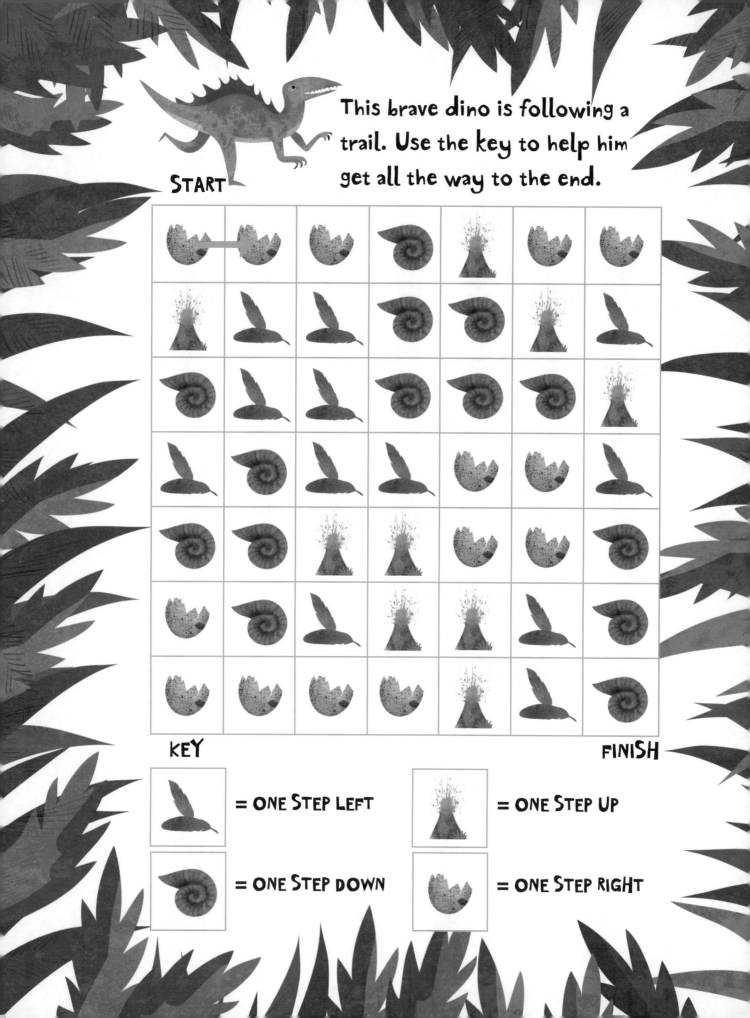

START

This brave dino is following a trail. Use the key to help him get all the way to the end.

KEY

FINISH

= ONE STEP LEFT

= ONE STEP UP

= ONE STEP DOWN

= ONE STEP RIGHT

Bright eyes and **white teeth!**

Complete the crazy dinosaur twins.

Draw a wild and wonderful view for this dinosaur to enjoy!

Create a cool comic strip story. Ready, steady, doodle!

THERE ONCE WAS A VERY SHY DINOSAUR ...

ROOARRRRR!

THE DINOSAUR RUSHED OUT OF HIS CAVE . . .

THE END

T. rex has **terrible** claws and **terrible** jaws!

Sketch him a set of teeth to **flash** and **snap**.

Draw some more bones for T. rex to **gnash** and **gnaw**!

Stare at this page for **60** seconds.
Try to remember everything you see.

Now turn over . . .

Cast your mind back to remember . . .

1
How many purple dinosaurs were there?

2
What color was the slithery snake?

3
How many ancient dragonflies did you see?

4
What color were the Pterosaur's wings?

5
How many horns did the Triceratops have?

6
What pattern was on the orange dinosaur's body?

When you've finished, color in this smart Stegosaurus!

Who's lurking in the deep, dark jungle?

These Pterosaurs are missing their wings! Color them in.

What creatures are lurking on this page? Read the clues, then draw a pair of dinosaurs that match the description.

I HAVE A BIG BODY.

1. There are spines on the end of my tail.

2. Armoured plates run all along my back.

3. I stand on four legs.

I AM TALL AND TOUGH.

1. I have tiny arms.

2. I stand on two legs.

3. My teeth are super-sharp.

BEWARE!

This volcano is going to blow!
Color in a path to solid ground.

START

FINISH

What a squish and a squeeze!

Let the dinosaur battle begin!

VERSUS

This **daring dinosaur** is hoping for a fish supper!

Can you spot five differences between these two pictures?

Eek! Diplodocus alert!
Doodle some tiny
dinosaurs darting
out of the way.

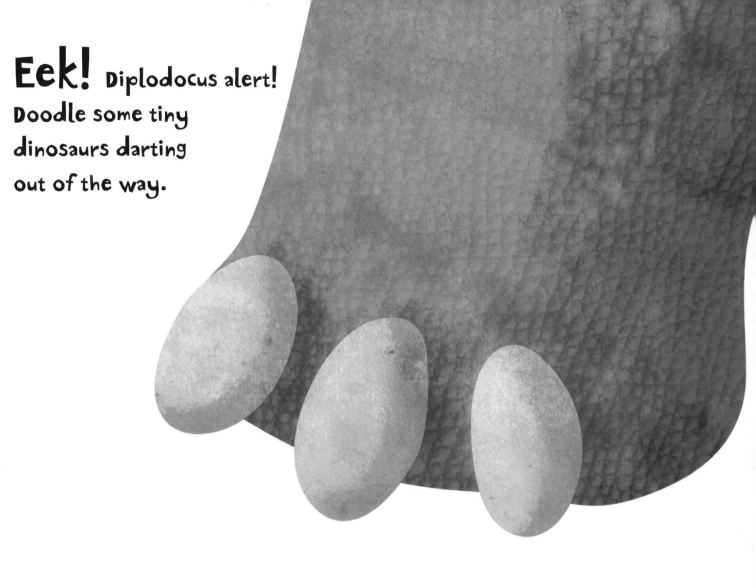

Use your doodling
skills to bring the
dinosaur herd to life.

Trudge! Stomp! Stamp!

Look at each row, then draw the next dinosaur in the sequence for each one.

Clawsome!

Cover this dinosaur in colorful patterns.

What has this sneaky snapper caught in its jaws?

Challenge a friend to this dinosaur coloring game!

You will need:
- **2 dice** (one for each player)
- a colored pencil each (make sure you each have different colors!)

Take turns to throw the dice.
If you throw an even number, color in one dinosaur.
If you throw a six, color in two dinosaurs.
If you throw an odd number, don't color any dinosaurs in.

Keep going until all of the dinosaurs are colored in.

The winner is the player with the most colored dinosaurs!

ROARR!

ROARR!

ROARRRR!

On your mark, get set, GO!

Draw, color, and doodle to give each dinosaur a matching mate.

Finish coloring in this **giant dinosaur!**

The forest is very quiet.

Who can you see in the trees?

Watch out!

This Pterosaur is swooping
down from the skies!

Add some flying friends!

Design a dinosaur! Sketch a brand-new species.

....
Write your dinosaur's name here.

Doodle a sleepy dinosaur gazing up at the Moon.

Night, night!